DEVELOPING INSTRUCTIONAL DESIGN

Geri McArdle, Ph.D.

CRISP PUBLICATIONS, INC.
Los Altos, California

DEVELOPING INSTRUCTIONAL DESIGN

Geri McArdle, Ph.D.

CREDITS
Editor: **Michael Crisp**
Layout and Composition: **Interface Studio**
Cover Design: **Carol Harris**
Cartoons: **Ralph Mapson**

Copyright © 1991 by Crisp Publications, Inc.
Printed in the United States of America

English language Crisp books are distributed worldwide. Our major international distributors include:

CANADA: Reid Publishing, LTD., Box 7267, Oakville, Ontario Canada L6J 6L6. TEL: (416) 842-4428, FAX: (416) 842-9327

AUSTRALIA: Career Builders, P. O. Box 1051, Springwood, Brisbane, Queensland, Australia 4127. TEL: 841-1061, FAX: 841-1580

NEW ZEALAND: Career Builders, P. O. Box 571, Manurewa, Auckland, New Zealand. TEL: 266-5276, FAX: 266-4152

JAPAN: Phoenix Associates Co., Mizuho Bldg. 2-12-2, Kami Osaki, Shinagawa-Ku, Tokyo 141, Japan. TEL: 3-443-7231, FAX: 3-443-7640

Selected Crisp titles are also available in other languages. Contact International Rights Manager Tim Polk at (415) 949-4888 for more information.

Library of Congress Catalog Card Number 90-83479
McArdle, Geri
Developing Instructional Design
ISBN 0-56052-076-0

PREFACE

Training With Success...''How-To-Do-It'' Book!

You can successfully train your employees or, improve your instructional performance. Do it quickly...easily, with this easy-to-follow book.

Results You Can Count On...

You will learn what to do to identify company training needs. Understand how tested training methods can work to make employees work harder and with greater determination to master learning materials. Step-by-step, you will learn how to choose the best training methodologies, tools and techniques. How to set realistic objectives. How to make your presentations exciting and easy-to-understand. Lastly, how to build the three critical factors of involvement, participation, and self-pacing into your training programs.

This Book Reveals...

- How to use a system to design a training program
- How to develop learning objectives
- How to evaluate and select training techniques
- How to plan and review your training program's performance
- How to identify objectives
- How to convert years of front-line experience into systematic, well-organized learning programs
- How to develop easy-to-follow presentation skills

Instruction design means using a systematic process to understand a human performance problem, figuring out what to do about it and finally, doing something about it.

This book is the trainer's survival kit, and is for anyone faced with designing and delivering training programs. The skills and technique, quizzes and checklists provide instant learning and feedback. You are now on your way to designing and presenting guaranteed successful training programs.

i

ABOUT THE AUTHOR

Geri McArdle, Ph.D., is managing director of Training Systems Institute, a training consulting group. She is an international award-winning author and Outstanding Faculty Member (1989) at The Johns Hopkins University and a postdoctoral fellow at Harvard University. Her latest two-book series is *Technical Training for Managers* and *Training for Teachers* (Fall, 1990). McArdle is contributing editor for the National Society for Performance and Instruction Journal and a consultant to General Electric, Xerox Corporation, CitiBank, the Department of State, and the White House. She has written seven books, produced public service television programs, and is a frequent international lecturer and guest faculty member teaching faculty and physicians. She welcomes questions or comments: TSI, 11490 Links Drive, Reston, Virginia 22090; telephone: (703) 435-1182.

DEDICATION

To Mike Crisp for his faith, Dr. Pete Petersen, of Johns Hopkins University to whom this draft is dedicated and to my Hopkins students who sold copies of my instructor's notes to fellow students as a study guide and thus began this writing journey.

Also I want to recognize Dr. H.H. Kaiser, of Syracuse University who formulated the design, my Mom who is always standing by, George Ordione, Mr. M.B.O., who commented on the initial draft and encouraged my simple style. And finally to Alice Dowsett and Kathleen Barcos supreme editors who keep me on a short leash!

CONTENTS

SECTION *I*

OVERVIEW

OVERVIEW

What is Instructional Design?

Instructional design simply defined means using a systematic process to understand a human performance problem, figuring out what to do about it and then doing something about it.

Why is Instructional Design Important?

If you've conducted or attended training programs, you've probably noticed that some are well planned, using an instructional design, while others are thrown together. If you are responsible for a program, don't waste time and money. Begin by developing an appropriate instructional design that will greatly increase your chances for training success.

Three reasons for developing an instructional program are:

1. To deliver new knowledge

2. To build skills

3. To change attitudes

This book provides an easy-to-follow, self-instructional design model that will guide you through the planning, preparing, conducting, and evaluating process of instructional design. It will incorporate the three reasons for training program development. If you follow each step of the four-step model presented, you will be able to design a successful training program in about an hour.

Why This Book?

Developing Instructional Design teaches practical instructional design techniques. These techniques make up the four-step instructional design model outlined later. This model will guide you through the process of creating an instructional design, developing learning objectives, selecting an instructional approach to your topic, preparing lesson outlines, and managing the learning experience.

OVERVIEW (Continued)

What is the Four-Step Model?

The instructional design process is a four-step cyclic activity. Simply met it involves planning which leads to preparing. Preparing permits conducting, and that requires evaluating learner progress. These basic activities (planning, preparing, conducting, and evaluating) establish the Four-step model:

STEP 1—PLANNING

Planning is the most important step in developing instructional design. It establishes the design framework. Planning means formulating the learning objectives, analyzing the training situation, outlining the body, and determining the method, sequence, and instructional approach.

STEP 2—PREPARING

Preparing is structuring your topic information in a written framework, which includes an introduction, a main body, a conclusion, and a summary. You must also consider styles of training delivery and rhetorical devices to respond to audience participation and questions.

STEP 3—CONDUCTING

The conducting activity is the action portion of the design. This is where everything you designed comes alive. Here is also where you should have developed and planned to use cues and other support materials to present a comprehensive and cohesive training design.

STEP 4—EVALUATING

The evaluating activity consists of trainer-directed activities to measure the trainee's understanding of the materials. These evaluation activities range from the informal ''trainer asks a question—trainee nods head'' to the formal written examination.

REVIEW—OVERVIEW

Reflecting on Our Perspectives

Reread the overview. Then return to this page and, without looking back, jot down 8-10 words that describe key things you are about to learn from this book.

_____

_____

_____

_____

_____

_____

_____

_____

Now, jot down three sequences of decisions you make in your daily life to get things done. Examples might be choosing what to wear in the morning or organizing a dinner party. Feel free to construct your own sequence.

_____	_____	_____
_____	_____	_____
_____	_____	_____
_____	_____	_____
_____	_____	_____
_____	_____	_____

SECTION II

STEP 1—
PLANNING

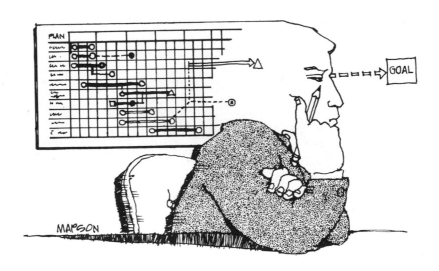

MARSON

STEP 1—PLANNING

Planning an instructional design is like planning to take a trip. You must decide where you want to go, gather your resources, consult a trip map, select a route, and get started. Like a trip map, developing an instructional design can be made easy if you use the newswriter's formula of What, Who, When, Where, Why and How.

Objectives are the first step in your journey in determining *what* is to be done, then incorporating *why* you are doing the training, and *how* you've done it right!

The first thing to do is to prepare well-stated learning objectives. There are three reasons for developing well-stated learning objectives: to guide the topic development by determining *what* is to be presented; to insure that you and the trainees will understand *why* the training is taking place; to establish for you, the trainer, *how* to evaluate the success of the training program.

Formulating an Objective defines the information or action you want the trainee to learn. A training objective consists of: purpose, topic, and desired result.

Purpose — Do you wish to inform or move the trainees to take specific action? Determine the purpose (make sure it fits the sponsor's intention) and keep this intent in mind during your design and presentation.

Topic — The topic must be stated clearly and specifically so everyone knows what the training is all about. Determine the depth of your information based on the needs of the group to be trained and on the time available. Make sure the level of training is clearly stated.

Desired Result — The desired results of the training must be part of your stated training objective. Results, which will depend on the needs of the trainees, could include:

1. To be familiar with the topic, basically understand the topic, to ask logical questions about it, and to keep up with discussions on it

2. To be informed enough to talk about the topic and to inform others about it

3. To be persuaded to take a specific action. If the purpose of your training is to move trainees to some action, make sure that the group understands clearly what you wish them to do.

EXAMPLES OF FORMULATING AN OBJECTIVE (Continued)

EXAMPLES:

You may wish your trainees to be informed.

Purpose: to teach

Topic: a new inventory system

Desired Result: so that trainees can understand and explain the system to others

This example is for a more academic approach: the information or knowledge is presented for its own sake. No subsequent action or testing is required.

You may wish your trainees to take action.

Purpose: to teach

Topic: a new inventory system and its application

Desired Result: so that the trainees can change their behavior to start using the new system in two weeks.

The major decision you make in developing this training design is determining to what extent the action is to be performed. For example, in teaching the use of a calculator, you can't expect the trainee to find the square root of a number in the first three minutes of learning the calculator's operations.

In developing your learning objectives, you must also consider why you are doing the training and how you are going to present this topic.

Why: Determine why this training is being sponsored. Remember the three reasons for designing training programs: to introduce new knowledge, to build skills or to change attitudes. Determine the precise expectations the sponsor has for you and what specifically your responsibility is to the three reasons for presenting training.

How: This is determined by the topic, your experience, background and experience of the group to be trained, and your instructional design. The how, or presentation of your topic, is preplanned. Adjustments to the design occur only to fit the audience need and not just because you feel like doing something different. Think of the overall training plan. Adjustments to the plan can be beneficial but only if the change is considered within the training design.

REVIEW

Reflecting and Recalling:

Without looking back, jot down what you think the three reasons are for establishing objectives:

1. _____

2. _____

3. _____

What is the most important determination to be made concerning the outcome of your training program?

The most important thing is to decide to _____

_____

What are the key critical elements to establishing sound objectives?

_____

_____

_____

ANALYZING THE SITUATION

Analyzing the situation involves answering the other questions in the formula: who is the audience, when will the training take place, and where is the training site.

In establishing an instructional design, you must first analyze the learning situation. You do this by determining your topic and subtopic areas; by researching the topics, framework, and audience; and then, if necessary, rewriting your learning objectives. Remember, you must understand as much as possible about the group to be trained and the overall situation that your training is to fit.

WHO: Know the game plan and other players. Who will introduce you? What names do you need to mention in your presentation, such as special individuals who are good references or role models? Who is the audience? The group to be trained is your most important component when preparing an instructional design. Are there any special groups or factors to remember? Consider all factors to help you shape an instructional design that will be appropriate for your audience needs: age, education, seniority, ethnic mix, etc.

Avoid verbal pitfalls by constructing last-minute safety checks. Situations may arise in which certain actions or statements from your training design would be inappropriate. Identify someone on site to fill you in on the traps of the organization's culture.

WHEN: Confirm the precise date, starting time, length, and occasion. If other speakers or trainers will take part, consider in what order will you speak. Determine what is going on before and after your training. Will you have to compete with after-lunch drowsiness, or are you scheduled for the final 20 minutes before the program ends? If this is the case, you may actually get only five or 10 minutes to talk. Consider what special attention-getting efforts you may have to use.

WHERE: Make sure you have the complete address, building identification, room location, and if necessary, special instructions for getting there and getting past security and into the training facility. The right facility can lead to your training success. An inappropriate or bad facility can lead to your downfall. Consider the following:

➡ *Site:* What does the training room look like? Check the seating, lighting, and temperature before you begin the training.

➡ *Location and Directions:* Determine ahead of time where the facilities are located; any special directions such as the restrooms, entrances, the closest telephone, photocopying machine, parking or unloading facilities, and emergency service.

➡ *Facilities:* Will you be in a hotel, lecture hall, classroom, restaurant, or auditorium? Will there be a problem with notetaking or line-of-sight to your visual aids? How are the chairs arranged? Can they be rearranged if need be?

➡ *Room Arrangement:*
Things that must be prearranged are the room arrangements for both you and the trainees. Consider the following list of items:

Elevation—will the group be looking up or down at you? Where can you best display your visual aids?

Room Shape—does the shape of the room hinder the most effective use of your visual aids?

Room Size—is the room the right size for your group? Can you change rooms if your audience size changes?

Availability—how much time will you have to prepare the facilities before your training? How much time can you spend after the training answering questions?

Equipment— do you need a projector, whiteboard, tables, etc.? If you have viewgraph slides, will there be a table on which you can place the slides while they are not in use? Are you familiar with the equipment? Will there be an opportunity to test it? Are back-up bulbs, etc., available in case of equipment failure?

Finally, here are some things that you may never think about, yet that are important in the planning stage.

Foreknowledge of the topic: How much does the group already know about your topic? Their knowledge and interest will help you determine the depth of material you must cover. Estimate in this planning phase your time for mingling among your group before the training program to establish rapport and determine the personal interests of your audience.

Number: How many people will attend? Get estimates of the audience in numbers, not adjectives. A ''few'' may imply five to you, but to your sponsor it may mean 50. You will be more comfortable if you know there will be 100 people out there, than if you find 100 when you weren't expecting more than 10.

ANALYZING THE SITUATION (Continued)

Vocabulary: Keep in mind the level of your audience. The fastest way to make an exciting subject boring is to talk over everyone's head. Training is not a time to see how many impressive words you know. Also, try not to use acronyms or initials unless you're sure everyone knows them. Try to use nontechnical terms, comparisions, and contrasts which the group can easily understand.

Verbal Pitfalls: Situations arise in which certain actions or statements from your training design would be inappropriate. Identify someone on site to fill you in on traps of the organization's culture.

Gather as much information as possible before you complete your instructional design, and check the design again with your contact shortly before the training takes place. This is also the best time to prepare your rhetorical devices for answering questions. Remember, think of the entire planning task as very important survival homework!

KEEP THE LEVEL OF YOUR AUDIENCE IN MIND

REVIEW

Reflecting and Recalling

You have just read about issues you need to consider before they become major problems.

Without looking back, how many can you recall? List as many items as you can below. (They don't have to be key terms, just thoughts you may forget as you step to the front of the room to start your program.)

_____	_____	_____
_____	_____	_____
_____	_____	_____
_____	_____	_____
_____	_____	_____

Now reread the last section to discover which elements you might have overlooked. Imagine which ones might make you anxious for a moment, just as you're being introduced!

_____

_____

_____

_____

_____

_____

_____

_____

PLANNING EXERCISE

Try this exercise. This page is divided by a line. Above the line, list the elements of a bad training situation you have (or might have) experienced, either as a trainer or as a participant.

Below the line, describe briefly a training situation (site, time, facitilites, audience size and composition) where you might feel most comfortable. If you like, start with a room and group of people you're already familiar with.

Elements of a bad training situation that I have encountered:

Description of a training situation in which I would feel comfortable:

CHOOSING AN EFFECTIVE TITLE

A title should be clear and simple. It should reflect your objectives. If your training program has a mandated title, keep it. Consider a subtitle that would simplify it. For example, if you are given something like, "An Examination of the Public School System and Its Roles in the Inculcation of Societal Norms," you can easily add a subtitle such as, "What are Jack and Jane *really* Learning in School?" The title and description of a program should be as creative, clear, and interesting as possible.

Many trainers use a working title for an instructional design until they have finished the preparation stage. This provides a picture of the training program as a whole. Furthermore, it provides a better chance of creating a title that best reflects the topic material and the basic approach of the training program. The "best" title reflects both what you are trying to say *and* the benefit it offers the learner. Try to develop a title that piques the learner's interest. It is difficult to build up enthusiasm for a presentation if the title puts everyone to sleep.

If at all possible, develop a title that informs and moves the learner. If you are training on time management, do not title your presentation, "Time Management." Everyone will get that much of the point throughout your talk. Say something more like, "You Deserve 10 Free Hours A Week." With a title such as this everyone will be looking for the proof of its assertion.

AVOID FLOWERY TITLES

REVIEW

Reflecting and Creating

Make up two catchy titles (or a title and a subtitle) for training programs on the following topics:

Basic Auto Repair For Women _____

_____

_____

How To Tell If A Baby Is Sick _____

_____

_____

How To Get Promoted _____

_____

_____

How To Price A House For Quick Sale _____

_____

_____

Electing the President _____

_____

_____

Write your titles on a separate sheet of paper and show them to someone who is not a trainer. Ask your friend what you would talk about and whether he or she would sit for an hour to hear you do so!

DEVELOPING THE BODY OF THE PRESENTATION

By now you have resolved the situation issues, and you are ready to start writing the body of your instructional design. Like an architect, it is necessary first to design the frame of the building. The title is the exterior form and presentation of the building, while the instructional design of the presentation is the basic structural frame. The outline controls the evolution of your training presentation.

In outlining the body of your instructional design, you must consider the following seven elements:

1. Developing your topic

2. Selecting an approach

3. Determining the sequence you will use to present the material

4. Selecting your method of presentation

5. Writing the major points of your lecture

6. Providing support for those points

7. Organizing the body.

In the next few pages we'll look at each of these seven elements separately.

REVIEW

Reflecting and Creating

I. List three broad areas, such as sports, gardening, and vacations, that are of interest to you and about which you have a fair amount of general knowledge:

_____   _____

_____   _____

_____   _____

Now note to the right how many one-hour sessions in a week you think you could spend giving informal presentations to friends on each topic.

Imagine that you are given 1½ hours to present the topic of your choice, and your boss (or supervisor) will be among the group attending. What immediately went through your mind before you chose a topic?

_____

_____

_____

_____

Having chosen a topic, choose a title, list five points that you feel are essential to cover, and think up a "clincher conclusion" (your favorite point) that will send them away at the end of the hour "positively buzzing."

Title: _____   points: _____

_____

_____

_____

_____

Clincher: _____

II. Think of two frequent topics of discussion at lunch (or at the coffee machine) between you and your co-workers, such as how to improve your promotability or tennis game or how to win a negotiation.

_____

_____

Now list the aspects, joys, concerns, strategies, etc. that you most often found yourself thinking about for one of these topics.

_____   _____

_____   _____

State what you think your objective is in bringing up this subject (or leaping into the debate when someone else brings it up).

> HINT: to brag about how much better you could do, to persuade your co-workers that someone is really unfit for their position, to inspire someone to an action that might change the situation.

_____

Stop and think about how Part II of this exercise differs from Part I in terms of such factors as others' guaranteed level of interest and pre-established time constraints. What do you notice?

_____

_____

_____

_____

_____

_____

_____

_____

Reflecting and Choosing

Select one topic from each of your answers to Part I and II of the preceding exercise. Examine each one using the journalist's criteria:

I	II
Topic: _____	Topic: _____
Who:	
What:	
Where:	
When:	
Why:	
How:	

SEVEN ELEMENTS TO PREPARE THE BODY

Element #1. Develop the Topic

The topic and the learning objective are interrelated. The topic tells you what the subject and point of the presentation is, and the objective tells you how deeply it will be covered. One of the major problems of long, boring presentations is the lack of a well-defined topic. Study the objectives below. If you had an hour to do your training program, which would you pick?

Broad Objective: To inform the audience about the government of Sydney, Australia.

Broad Topic: The government of Sydney, Australia. This topic could include the entire governmental structure, past, present, and future of Sydney, Australia.

Limited Objective: To inform the training group about the director for transportation in Sydney.

Limited Topic: Director of transportation in Sydney, Australia and assigned duties.

An obvious advantage of the limited topic is that it also provides some direction for researching your topic: information about duties of the director of transportation services in Sydney, Australia.

The broad topic clearly needs some limitation; e.g., specific agencies in government, time frame, political factors, products, or services.

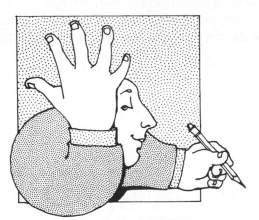

BROAD OBJECTIVE
BROAD TOPIC
LIMITED OBJECTIVE
LIMITED TOPIC

SEVEN ELEMENTS (Continued)

Element #2. Decide on an Approach

Now that you have limited your topic, you need to consider what facets of the topic you will cover and what questions you will answer. What exactly do you want to tell your training group? While there are a great number of approaches, some of which are quite creative, let us turn to that of the newspaper writer. Applying it to our topic, we get to choose from the following:

WHO: Who are the people, agencies, or offices that provide the transporation service? Also, who needs their services and who is eligible?

WHAT: What transportation services are offered or not offered?

WHERE: Where are the transportation requests processed?

WHEN: When did the agency begin operation (history of the organization)?

WHY: Why is Sydney offering these services?

HOW: How does the director decide which policies or programs are most important or most effective?

As you can see, more than one approach may be used. You may decide to answer all of the questions; given enough time, you probably could. Especially if you know your subject well, the time allotted to you will probably be insufficient to say all you really want to say. The successful trainer is one who, given a set amount of time, decides on just what is needed and presents only the most important information.

Element #3. Determine the Sequence

The corollary to the approach is the sequence. In what order should you present your materials after you have gathered the information? Generally, writers and researchers follow the journalist's prescription in this range of sequences:

WHO:	From top to bottom of an organizational structure, famous to unknown, most highly visible to anonymous.
WHAT:	From familiar to unfamiliar, frequent to infrequent, or in a case of problem solving—from problem to solution.
WHERE:	Directional, from north to south, or east to west, from the field to the main offices.
WHEN:	From some point in the past to a current time and on to the future. For a short period—one month—or a longer one—10 years.
WHY:	From a statement of the importance or relevance of a problem to its resolution.
HOW:	Procedures or process, step by step.

These are only general recommendations. Select the most logical sequence—one that you feel best serves the purpose of your training.

REVIEW

Reflecting and Conditioning

Reconsider your two favorite topics—those that might make the most sense (and be most interesting) for a 30-minute talk. If necessary, jot down several angles from the journalist's criteria, write out possible sequences, and compare them to the others.

WHO:

WHAT:

WHERE:

WHEN:

WHY:

HOW:

Element #4. Select a Method

The next step is to determine how best to present your material to the audience. There are three most commonly used methods of instructional design:

1. **A series of facts.** You state facts and supply information to back them up. This is most effective if the audience is already familiar with your topic.

2. **A series of comparing or contrasting statements or questions.** In essence, put your audience in a forced-choice position: "Would you rather build a poultry industry in District X or send them food shipments in 1998?" This method is most effective when your objective is to inform. If informing is your goal, weigh information so your desired outcome is obvious. You want the learners to understand or know something specific. The downside to this is that not everyone thinks certain things are as obvious as you think they are (and not everyone may agree with your conclusion—but more on that later).

3. **A series of questions.** Several techniques are involved here. You may ask a question, then:

   a. Give a direct answer and provide proof

   b. Provide proof and let the audience draw a conclusion (preferably yours)

   c. Prompt the audience for the correct answer.

To make any of these methods work, you must use the main points or facts that you want to make in your training presentation. Do not waste time on minor or obsure facts: drive home your point.

REVIEW

Reflecting and Constructing

Go back to the five essential points you isolated in Part I's exercise for your presentation. Add five more that you think could be helpful in getting your point or explanation across.

PRINCIPAL POINTS/ISSUES   **SECONDARY POINTS/ISSUES**

_____   _____

_____   _____

_____   _____

_____   _____

Now use the threee methods presented to decide how you want to order and package all points. You may use different methods for sub-groupings of fact, but remember, you only have 60-90 minutes and complexity takes more time to present clearly than consistent use of one method. As you work with longer presentation periods and gain more experience in planning, you can build in a larger variety of methods.

Element #5. Write Down the Main Points

The main points in an instructional design are those that lead the trainee to the learning objective of the trainer. To return to our example of designing a building, the main points are the stress-bearing walls. They hold up the entire argument of the design.

When preparing your main points:

1. Include all materials necessary to reach the objective. The key word here is *necessary*; avoid vague or unrelated materials.

2. Organize the main points in the sequence you will use to present them.

3. Present the main points in the form of sentences, using the method you have decided upon; i.e., statements or questions.

4. Limit the main points: four is usually considered a workable number. List only main points, double-checking to make sure they are independent of each other and not just different facets of the same point.

REVIEW

Reflecting and Composing

Look again at the main points you have chosen for your sample one-hour, informal lunch talk. Write out each one. Then look at them again and try to choose four.* This is not a strict number, but a guideline for building a balanced presentation and setting out guideposts that your audience can lean on—and remember! Make sure they all are of comparable importance, otherwise you have a lopsided (and crumbing) building. If necessary, demote one or two and find others—or raise a secondary point to a primary level of importance.

My Main Points Are:

_____

_____

_____

_____

_____

_____

_____

_____

_____

_____

_____

_____

Element #6. Support the Main Points

After you have listed your main points, it is time to do your research and support them with information. The best support system is one based on different types of facts, in a variety of forms.

Support must come in the form of interesting information: you can't prove a point if the audience loses attention because of saturation or boredom during your training. Choose interesting, closely related, short, crisp facts in developing your training modules, and present them in a variety of forms: For instance:

Straight facts:

According to the Department of Commerce, Mexico was the largest generator of travel revenue for the United States in 19XX.

Statistics to prove the point:

In 19XX, visitors from Mexico spent $.4 billion in the United States.

Quotations to support a viewpoint:

"Our goal is to encourage our friends across the border to come to the United States and build better political and business relationships." (San Diego mayor, 1900)

Comparisons that relate the topic to the training group:

Welcoming foreign visitors is like having your favorite aunt come and visit: you make them welcome, then you just sit back and have fun.

Humorous or serious narratives about people and events:

The travel group from Japan that wanted to try American food, ate pizza, tacos, and sushi!

Questions, generally rhetorical, with answers may help track down your point:

"Do you know what the least known export is from the United States? Tourism! Last year it brought in more than $11 billion in receipts! We could reduce the national deficit if the tourism business were further developed!"

All of the above examples are great for openers. Using any of the openers, however, must be appropriate and directly related to your training module. The openers are "interest teasers" and a preview of the real issues to be discussed in the body of your training presentation. The above examples are specific openers for a customer service or travel industry representing Mexico.

REVIEW

Reflecting and Complementing

Take two main points from your sample topic (and two secondary ones, if you're feeling ambitious) and try to find a way to support each one using each of the suggested techniques:

MAIN POINTS	SECONDARY POINTS
Straight Fact _____	**Straight Fact** _____
_____	_____
_____	_____
_____	_____
Statistics _____	**Statistics** _____
_____	_____
_____	_____
_____	_____
Quotation (make one up!) _____	**Quotation** _____
_____	_____
_____	_____
_____	_____
Real-life Comparison _____	**Real-life Comparison** _____
_____	_____
_____	_____
_____	_____
Anecdotal Example _____	**Anecdotal Example** _____
_____	_____
_____	_____
_____	_____

GATHERING INFORMATION

Gathering information can be fun, but don't let it get out of hand. In order for your training presentation to be most effective, balance your presentation so the audience stays interested. Use different forms, but don't overdo it. Some rules to consider:

➡ In the instructional design, use cues in your trainer notes. This avoids the impression that you're reading and gives a more spontaneous effect. To achieve this, you must design your material so that it has a logical flow and some key sentences or phrases that are used as introductions and transitions throughout the design. This creates continunity and topic focus.

➡ In using quotes in your materials or instructional technologies, copy them *exactly* as the original, but place them in quotation marks.

➡ If your objective is to inform the audience enough to make them able to talk about your topic, you can use audience participation to reinforce your major points.

➡ Write down all statistics, numbers, formulas, and complex amounts on the flip chart. Round off large numbers and keep statistics as simple as possible. Guard against obvious arithmetic errors since someone will surely be checking your figures. Work all problems ahead of time, in the design phase, to ensure that they make the point you are trying to make and that they work!

➡ Stay on the technical level of the audience. When in doubt, better too simple than too complex in the design of the topic.

SEVEN ELEMENTS (Continued)

Reflecting and Reviewing

Whether you have been working straight through this manual—all at one go—or doing it in parts and maybe building a training plan as you read, close it for a minute, take a deep breath, and try to recall some of the principal elements that go into constructing an effective training plan. Jot them down if that helps.

Now, go back to the table of contents and check to see how much you've retained. Don't worry if you feel you've flunked your own quiz: this is meant to be a guide and reference to be kept by your side and consulted at will. (It will be like an open-book research paper until you get to your first training session, at which time you'll be in the spotlight with only your crib notes—your training plan—to glance at occasionally.

If some of the sections or subsections in the table of contents seem oddly familiar, now is the time to reread those parts carefully, consult the table of contents again to re-establish your perspective, and move on. This is an important exercise, not only in your own process of learning and assimilation (much of which will, of course, come through practice), but also as a reminder that you will need to have your audience stop and review—periodically and just before the end—lest they end up after a few hours or days losing track of the big picture and its various parts. Studies have shown that the average adult's *maximum* span of attention-concentration-learning tends to be 1½ hours. As much as you can, you should plan your modules, review steps, question periods, and breaks around this factor.

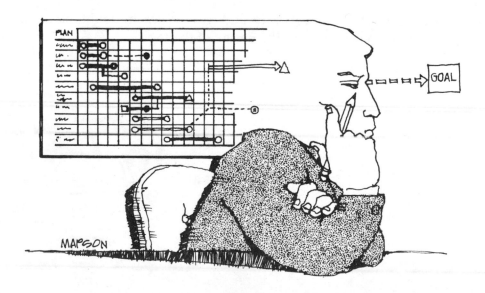

Element #7. Organize the Body

In designing instruction we all reach this point of having copious notes, piles of overdue books, and a mountain of relevant magazines and articles. Now comes the fun part—selecting and organizing your material. Check each step once it has been completed.

COMPLETED   STEP

☐　　　**1.** Pick out the material you want to use. Keep referring to your topic and your objectives; throw out anything that is not immediately useful. (Or, if you wish, save it for another presentation.) Select the information that you think will have the greatest appeal to your audience. Keep in mind the need for variety and change of pace. One good rule is to limit yourself to no more than four major points that support your main training topic.

☐　　　**2.** Estimate how much of the material it will take to fill 80% of your presentation time. Estimate—it's too soon to rehearse. After you've done this a few times, you will be surprised at how accurate your estimates become.

☐　　　**3.** Put all your support-information cues in order for your training presentation. List them in order of importance and number to prevent confusion during the module writing stage. Support materials should be in the same sequence as the main points so you can find them.

Review the list of materials. Begin to build your training modules. Separate the materials and place them into separate stacks. Now you can start to write your training module. Remember, begin with your primary topic module first, then your last module. Fill in the middle modules as your last step.

REVIEW

Reflecting and Connecting

Think of some key words or phrases that you would like to use repeatedly to hold the sections together and remind your audience from where you've come and where you're headed. Don't overdo the ''thus and therefore...'' but, just as hikers need to stop, catch their breath, and check the map, your audience will need pauses and familiar ''landmarks'' to help stay on the trail with you.

DEVELOP PRESENTATION AIDS

Sometimes it becomes evident that words and gestures are not going to be enough to get the message across. In that case, the design requires supplementary aids. The operative word is supplementary: aids should be used only to enhance the message, to make it more memorable, not to deliver it. You are the only one who will get to take them home for a second look!

There are five reasons to use supplementary aids:

1. When a point is too complex for spoken words alone. Words can be misunderstood more easily than simple pictures.

2. When the point calls for a specific visual image—i.e., the machine you are describing.

3. When you are working for a higher level of retention. People grasp and remember visual images much more easily than intellectual arguments.

4. When you need to retain the group's attention or to get everyone to the same point or conclusion.

5. When you need to summarize, especially if you are attempting to pull several points together, the old adage really does apply: ''A picture is worth a thousand words.''

DEVELOPING PRESENTATION AIDS
(Continued)

Three Instruction Technologies

1. **Object Aids:** All three-dimensional objects, including people and animals, qualify as object aids. You, the trainer, can serve as an excellent aid: drastic voice changes, dramatic movements, calculated posture, even your clothing can serve as aids. Members of the audience may also be aids if you can present them as good examples. One of the aids we're most familiar with is the demonstration of sample goods.

2. **Projected Aids:** These aids require equipment and include images projected on a screen such as movies and slides and sound devices such as tape recorders. These often require the assistance of a technician, so think through the reason for this aid, and make sure the extra help is available.

3. **Nonprojected Aids:** Topics that require showing tables, charts, lists, diagrams, or maps are obvious examples of nonprojected aids. They range from formal or professional graphics to the stick figures you draw. These aids may be presented on an easel with a paper pad, felt board, peg board, magnet board, or whiteboard. Beware of depending on exhibits that you hand out before your training presentation. People will tend to keep their eyes on your handouts rather than on you!

All instructional aids should be used sparingly. They are supplemental information and should support your training, not deliver it. You are the expert and you have the experience that is to be shared. Aids exist to reinforce your points. They are most effectively used as cues, keys to help you remember what you want to describe.

At the same time, they help your trainees grasp your points through memorable visual or aural images (remember that TV jingle you can't get out of your head?). In fact, if your trainees could also touch, smell, and taste your exhibits, they would probably never forget them!

REVIEW

Reflecting and Relining

Stop and recall any training presentations you may have observed—or been subjected to! Were aids used? List some of the kinds you've seen, using our three groups. Which seemed to be most effective? Does recalling a particular visual bring back to you the purpose of the training or a particular point the trainer was trying to make? If so, it was clearly an effective one for that time and place. Make a note of it for yourself, for similar uses you might have in your presentation.

Aids I have observed during a presentation (list as many as you can):

1. _____

2. _____

3. _____

4. _____

5. _____

6. _____

7. _____

8. _____

9. _____

10. _____

11. _____

12. _____

The most unusual aid I have seen during a presentation was:

_____

_____

PRELIMINARY EVALUATION

At this point, start considering how you will evaluate the effectiveness of your instructional design. Will it be necessary to test your audience, or can you build feedback and evaluation elements into the presentation?

For emphasis, remember that evaluation is really a test of your effectiveness. You, after all, know that you are the best qualified to teach the topic and proper prior planning makes a perfect presentation. Evaluation proves you did your job.

Evaluations or tests built into or following a training design may have a second purpose: to reinforce in the minds of your audience what they are learning (or will have learned). Careful! Few people like to take tests or be called on in class, and written exercises scheduled elsewhere than immediately before pauses can seriously damage your audience's attention span and the flow of your presentation.

"NOW FOR MY EVALUATION"

REVIEW

Reflecting and Reconstructing

Think back to your school days. Make a list of as many types of tests, interrogations, learning, or progress checks as you can remember.

1.

2.

3.

4.

5.

6.

Which ones made you feel uncomfortable (whether you knew the answers or not)? Which made you feel most at ease being called on when you had your hand up? Your audience will not be children, but some may well feel a bit intimidated or overwhelmed by all you've presented.

Avoid using form evaluations with only one type of question; e.g.,
Circle a number:
Not Effective   1   2   3   4   5   Effective

This form requires tabulation time and does not give you as thorough feedback as an assortment of types of questions or prompts. Many trainers use a form, or a blanket ''Tell me what you liked best and least'' form of evaluation, usually just before or just after the end of their presentation. To be effective, this sort of evaluation needs to be scheduled into your time allotted, preferably before you give your concluding remarks and thus before your audience starts thinking about other things.

SECTION *III*

STEP 2— PREPARING

STEP 2—PREPARING

Gathering the Building Blocks

You've collected all your information; you have an instructional design that contains your objectives, topic, and subtopic; now it's time to work on the preparation part of your presentation. In this section we will look at the art of preparing introductions, conclusions, and summaries. We will also learn about timing, sequencing, and revisions.

THE INTRODUCTION

Now you are ready to sit down and write your training presentation. You might have to write your presentation several times to make it your best and be in full control of it! Don't worry about the number of drafts: the important thing is to understand your focus, get a sense of the design, timing, and sequencing of the information. You are trying to establish the content and the rhythm for its presentation in your memory.

Take time in writing your introduction. The introduction is really the first time the participants meet you. Now is the time to make a great first impression. If you don't get their attention now, it will be difficult to hold their attention and have your information accepted. There are only three rules to follow when writing your introduction:

1. Write out the introduction completely for yourself. Usually the worst part of delivering a talk is the first few minutes. A written introduction will help you to get over the first awkward moments.

2. The introduction should only take about 10% of the speaking time. You should be able to explain the topic, state your objective, and hit the high points of the succeeding modules quickly.

3. Write the introduction for your audience. Keep it at level they can easily understand.

There is a bit of a trick you can use during the introduction period. Remember, this is your qualifying period, the time during which you establish yourself as an expert the audience should respect. You can cement this respect by asking the audience to perform some minor act according to your instruction. For instance, ask several of them to move forward to fill the front row (which is usually empty) and wait in expectant silence for them to do.

Generally, some will respond and many will not, but the activity you have directed adds just a little bit to your command stature. Be sure you select a task you are confident they will carry out. If you are one of several speakers, some other kind of task may be more appropriate, such as "stand up and stretch."

DESIGNING YOUR INTRODUCTION

In designing your introduction, know that an introduction has three major purposes:

1. **To acknowledge** your sponsor, to give some recognition to the company, group, or individuals who arranged the gathering, and to give some background about you: to establish your authority and reason for being there.

2. **To gain the attention** of the trainees and to motivate them to listen. One need not be a clown to gain attention; you could design a series of questions related to the modules that follow, a humorous story, or joke. An acknowledgement of the sponsor's current events might also be used. People want to listen to things that are of interest to themselves: figure out what they're interested in and tie your remarks to it. Any topic sentence can be fitted to a specific audience if you do your homework.

3. **To provide an overview** of the entire training presentation and let the trainees know what you hope to accomplish. Let the trainees see the objectives, and talk about the strategies you will be using. It's far easier to achieve your training objective if the audience knows what you are leading up to. This also sets the tone of the training. By stating up front the expectations for both the trainer and trainee, you reduce misunderstanding and disappointments.

REVIEW

Reflecting and Recalling

For each of these three purposes, try to think of one or two clever devices you've seen speakers use elsewhere in introductions. List them below—they might come in handy!

1. _____

_____

_____

_____

_____

2. _____

_____

_____

_____

_____

3. _____

_____

_____

_____

_____

THE CONCLUSION

The conclusion is your last pitch—this is what the trainees will be most likely to remember about your training presentation. The same rules apply to the conclusion as to the introduction. Write it out—this time to assure yourself of a strong conclusive ending. Make sure it lasts no more than 20% of your speaking time. Tell them why they needed this information and that you have established your point. Whether the audience remembers some particularly salient points or a terrific quote, viewgraph, or videotape—it's all up to you.

The three elements of the conclusion should do the following:

1. **Summarize your presentation.** You may want to review your main points and supporting material. Reiterate your strongest, most salient points. Do not bring in any new material.

2. **Motivate your audience.** Make the trainees glad they came to hear you. Take a few hard facts that apply personally to the audience and use them to reinforce your message. If your purpose was to inform the audience, take this chance to remind everyone why and specifically how to do what you want them to do.

3. **Close your presentation.** Develop a concise closing statement that will be pointed enough to be remembered when the training is over. If you know you have a question-and-answer period, be prepared to close twice, which will almost certainly be necessary.

Although your closing statement will be written out, you should practice delivering it often enough so it's almost memorized. This will help insure that it flows smoothly and that you won't have to read it with your nose in your notes—and thereby risk losing your audience's attention at such a critical moment!

THE CONCLUSION (Continued)

The Summary

The summary is distinct from the closing remarks. It may take the form of a printed handout or a one-page synopsis of the objectives and the important points covered in the training.

The summary should contain the title of the training, name of the trainer, and the date, time, and place. It should have the objectives of the training plainly stated. It must contain all the main points you covered and at least refer to the most important support material. This is where you should include the bibliography, if you have one.

Depending on the sponsoring organization, you may or may not want to mention them at the very end. In terms of quantity, always bring at least 10% more copies of your handouts than you expect to need.

Motivating Your Audience

If you did your homework thoroughly in preparing your training plan, you should already know some pertinent things about your audience. If you have received the occasional question during your presentation and if you have mingled with your trainees during breaks, you should know even more about them. You may also have noticed times when they brightened up, sat up, and took special interest in a point you made.

Figure out ahead of time a couple of catchy lines that will make each person feel your presentation has been directed at him or her personally. Others may occur to you in the course of your session. (''Well, I've enjoyed working with you'' is not enough.)

Closing

Develop some friendly, polite clinchers along the lines of: ''Today, we have learned X, and while I'll say good-bye, I trust you won't be saying 'farewell' to what you've learned in this session.''

REVIEW

Reflecting, Reviewing, and—Exit Stage Left

If you have been working up a fictitious or sample training plan as you've read through this manual, now is the time to go back over it and write your conclusion. Be sure to include the three parts.

Think back to presenters who brought their talks to a graceful and effective (or clumsy and ineffective) end. Write out one or two anecdotes, noting what the audience did well (or flubbed). If you've never been to a talk, speech, or presentation where the speaker had a specific overall point to get across and included a concluding section, try to find one to observe before you do a training plan and session of your own (at which time you will be the one being observed).

QUESTIONS AND ANSWERS

If the presentation is to include a question-and-answer period, particularly before a hostile audience, write out all the questions you might be asked. The best way to prepare for a difficult session is to anticipate. Think of all the awkward and pointed questions you may be asked and rehearse some stock answers.

Even if you must confess ignorance, say, ''The matter is still under study,'' or ''Let me get back to you on that.'' However, having considered the question beforehand will make you less likely to be trapped into saying or inferring something that can get you into real trouble.

Are there any particularly weak spots in your presentation upon which you expect to be questioned? If so, defuse the situation early. Bring up any weakness yourself and answer the expected question during your presentation. Do it early—you earn more points from trainees that way. Don't let the hostile questioner have the last say or it will destroy some of your credibility.

REHEARSALS AND REVISIONS

The best trainers rehearse and rehearse. A rehearsal is an excellent chance to check your terminology to be sure the audience will understand you, to time yourself, and to experiment with your voice, posture, gestures, and expressions.

You rehearse to:

1. **Check** terminology and content. Consider how much the trainees know about the topic. While you rehearse, take notice of any words or concepts that are not clear to you or that you have some trouble with. You may have to put more precise definitions in the revised version of your training materials.

2. **Time yourself.** Present each part of your training—introduction, body, conclusion—and watch the clock. Since you want to replicate as much as possible the actual presentation, you will need to go through the presentation out loud. Set up a training area, your presentation aids, a clock, and a pencil. As you finish each point of your lecture, write down the time. Talk through your speech out loud and use your aids. Experiment with your voice, practice a change in posture, or try out gestures that help emphasize your point. If you can, practice in front of someone else.

   - **Read** the introduction (You won't want to read it during the presentation unless your mind goes blank).

   - **Talk** through the body of your presentation using your cues.

   - **Present** all your aids.

   - **Read** the conclusion.

   - **Write** down the time spent with each portion, and total it all up. Make time for questions.

The instructional design and presentation should be revised for two things: vocabulary and time. The vocabulary revisions are fairly simple: take the words or concepts that you have noted as possible problems and either define them or select clearer substitutes. If you must use words that are way beyond the experience of your trainees, you may have to remind them of the definitions twice. Also, prepare a definition sheet, if you did not do so earlier in the design.

REHEARSALS AND REVISIONS (Continued)

To revise your timing is a little more difficult. First of all, remember the formula for the introduction and the conclusion; these sections together should make up 20% and certainly not more than 30% of your presentation time. Therefore, if you have a two-hour time limit, about 24 minutes should be spent on the introduction and the conclusion. That leaves 96 minutes for the body of the speech. (This does not include any time for questions and answers.) Now, to revise or fine-tune your timing, refer to the following quidelines:

Introduction:

- If your introduction is more than 10% of your speaking time, revise it by subtracting words and details.

- If your introduction is less than 10% of your speaking time, extend it by adding details or partially developing your points, but, in doing this, don't give one point more weight than it deserves in comparison to the others.

Body:

- If the body of the presentation takes more than 80% of the time, be more concise; keep major points and supporting materials but tighten everything up. Pay attention to the weight you are giving each of your main points.

- If the body is too short, make it longer by adding new support material; don't pad what you already have.

Conclusion:

- Revise your conclusion to fit 20% of your time using the same guidelines as for the introduction above.

The total time in minutes should be 95%–105% of the allowable speaking time. Some leeway is possible in the 10%–70%–20% formula. An absolutely perfect training presentation is an impossibility. Don't worry about it, revise as well as you can, then sit back and relax.

Something needs to be said here about on-site revisions. You can write a wonderful presentation, rehearse and time it perfectly, then run into snags when it's time to deliver it. In cases where something unexpected turns up, it is up to the trainer to determine if the presentation should include some new information or whether it should be amended or cut short. Be aware of your trainees and the situation.

LESSON PLAN FORMAT AND CHECKLIST

- **Title:** Descriptive and concise

- **Objectives:** Topic, purpose, desired results

- **References:** List all texts, readings, books, articles, reprints, etc.

- **Introduction:** To stimulate interest, motivate, state objectives, and establish the scope of the lesson. In the case of a series of meetings, it ties the current lesson to previous and following lessons. The introduction should only be 10% of the total presentation.

- **Body of Presentation:**
  1. Outline the subject matter
  2. Develop your approach, sequence, and method
  3. Select main points and supports
  4. Concentrate on how to make the lesson effective
     a. Talk on the level of the audience
     b. Encourage group participation
     c. Emphasize and repeat major points
     d. Push the group mentally by asking questions
     e. Use attention-getting presentation aids
     f. Involve the group in as many activities and interchanges as possible
     g. Change your position often, pitch your voice to give emphasis, use different gestures
     h. Appeal to as many senses as possible, and be creative: get your point across using your audience's sense of sight, hearing, taste, smell, or touch. Vary your communication techniques.

- **Audience Participation:** Historically, audiences have always participated by simply being there. Thanks to modern research into adult learning, we have established that people learn best by seeing and doing things. The lessons most easily learned and retained are those in which theory is immediately related to a group activity. Use structured exercises, including miniprojects, role-playing, special research efforts, or demonstrations, with individuals, small groups, teams, or the entire group. The exercises need not be elaborate, but the benefits are two-fold: the audience teaches itself by reinforcement, and the people who tend to sleep in the back have to stay awake.

LESSON PLAN FORMAT AND CHECKLIST
(Continued)

- **Conclusion:** The best conclusions are short and to the point. This is your last chance to take the information you have delivered, make it relevant to the group, and make them want to remember it. Once again, it should be about 20% of your presenting time.

- **Summary:** The summary gives you, the trainer, another chance at getting your message across:

  1. Outline all of your main points succinctly. If there is enough space, include the principal supports of your points.

  2. Make sure that any written outline follows your presentation and includes any reference readings.

  3. Use enough material in both the introduction and conclusion so the summary can stand alone, or if it is part of a series, tie it to the other presentations.

  4. If you are handing out summaries or class notes, have available at least 10% more than you think you will need.

REVIEW THE LESSON PLAN

Is it necessary for your training presentation to be reviewed by another? If your presentation involves organizational policy, you should have it reviewed by the proper authority. The whole presentation usually needs not be submitted, but the outline, plans for question-and-answer sessions, and any materials for distribution should be reviewed by someone in a position of authority. When the policy review is finished, revise as necessary. There should be no surprises in a training presentation and no inappropriate remarks made or facts revealed.

Complete the Final Draft

The final draft of your training presentation should include everything you want to take with you when you conduct your training. All parts of the lesson plan should be printed or typed, and the pages should be numbered so you can refer to your notes easily. Make sure you have all the information you need for the training, including visual aids cued to your lesson plan, visual aid equipment, and trainee handouts.

SECTION *IV*

STEP 3— CONDUCTING

STEP 3—CONDUCTING

Presenting the Program

The lesson plan is the road map for your training presentation. It documents the main points and supporting materials, presentation aids, and timing.

Preparing your lesson plan is similar to the materials prepared in Steps 1 and 2 because it once again gives you a standard logical format for your training presentation. The major difference is that the lesson plan covers a much more extended interaction between the trainer and trainees.

Using the Lesson Plan   Although the presentation plan is extremely useful for the one-time training presentation, it becomes rather tedious for someone who is teaching a series of the same courses. The lesson plan takes over.

Sometimes there are too many topics, as in a survey of Far Eastern cultures, or the needed depth is too great, such as a presentation on the sociology of one particular culture. In such cases, several meetings will be required. The lesson plan is the basic tool of the multitopic training. It is useful as a road map that tells you where you've been and gives an indication of where you are going.

A lesson plan, properly written, can be used by anyone to do the training. A substitute trainer must have some background in the topic, but the plan is not as closely identified with a particular person as the single training presentation.

FIVE LESSON PLAN COMPONENTS

The lesson plan is a simple presentation of all the facts and topic information needed to present the training. The information needed in developing each component is described below:

1. **Objectives:** Describe the criteria for acceptable performances and what the trainee will do when the training is completed.

2. **Heading:** Contains the title of the training and course, stated objective, total time required, methods, approach, sequence, presentation aids, trainee materials, equipment, and references.

3. **Introduction:** Grabs attention and motivates trainees. It ties in with the stated objectives and reasons why they should learn.

4. **Development:** Expands the main points: what trainees must learn to attain the objectives. It lists subpoints, time cues, instruction activities. It contains a logical breakdown of the tasks or information needed for accomplishing the objectives.

5. **Summary:** Reviews the main points and shows their relationship to the trainees. Additionally, it could tie one session of training into the next presentation. This is an opportunity to test the trainees to assess whether you reached your objectives or not.

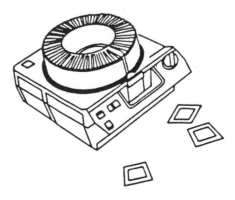

Determining Enabling Objectives Enabling or instructional objectives are those objectives that trainers set for their own use. The enabling objectives are useful in planning, ordering instructional activities, and evaluating the activities' effectiveness. The more clearly the objectives are defined, the easier it is to tell if they are being met. For example:

Program Objective: To teach a new technique of terrace farming to rice farmers in Borneo.

Instructional Objective: After each portion of a training module, trainees should be able to complete the following:

1. To describe terrace and other farming methods well enough so they can pass a short quiz.

2. To teach others how to identify the conditions under which the new technique could be used and to discuss it with the local agricultural committee.

3. To know enough about the new terrace technique so they could design a farming program for an area of 10, 100, 1,000, or 10,000 acres in Borneo.

The three major parts of the instructional objective include the following:

PART I   **Behavior or Performance:** The first portion of the instructional objective consists of the object and an action verb. The question asked of the trainer is, ''What does what?''

PART II   **Conditions:** This refers to the givens, circumstances, or restrictions that may apply to the case. The question asked is, ''Under what conditions do things get done?''

PART III **Criteria or Standards:** This refers to a measure of how well the action gets done. Factors considered may include completeness, quantity, quality, time, or accuracy. The question here is, ''How well must things be done to meet the objectives?''

Plan for Testing To judge the effectiveness of your training presentation, it is necessary to determine whether students have mastered the training objectives. This is done by measuring performance, or testing. Unfortunately, testing has a negative image for most people; in other words, people react badly to being tested—sometimes even when they only think they are being tested.

Testing, however, can be a positive, invaluable tool. The successful training presentations are those that are constructed so that objectives, major points, and important information are readily picked out and remembered after the training. It is up to the trainer to determine when and how to test; that is, to find out how well the trainer met the stated learning objectives.

Managing the Training Environment In each training situation several universal training problems may, and probably will, face the trainer. These problems range from having one disruptive participant to facing an entire hostile audience. This brings up again the importance of an audience analysis. While difficult to predict all problems, it is helpful to know before you present if individuals or groups will present problems.

Common Problems When Conducting Training Sessions

Problem 1. Noncommunicative group or individuals

Solutions
1. Ask direction questions to the group.
2. Ask yes/no questions to individuals, then follow with a why question. It helps to call the individual by name, if possible.
3. Restate or reword questions or statements to focus attention and elicit responses.
4. Rethink the audience's motivation for attending, state it aloud, and show how it really relates to what you have to say.

Problem 2. Compulsive, insistent talker

Solutions
1. Ask direct yes/no summarizing questions, thank the trainee, and move back to your presentation. This will help the trainee to feel that their point was made.
2. Offer to relay follow-up questions to someone outside of the presentation. Make the offer specific so the questioner does not feel put off if you state you are not the expert on that issue, yet can find out.
3. Suggest that you get together outside the lecture or after the presentation. Offer to set the time and place right after the presentation.
4. Take the trainee aside at break and discuss the effect they are having on the group. Be tactful, but firm.

Problem 3. You lose control of the presentation

Solutions
1. Re-establish eye contact. Deliberately and carefully look each person in the eyes in turn as you speak. Direct their eyes to you and to your visuals by your actions. If you have dimmed the room lights for visuals, turn them on brightly.
2. Change your position, stand up, sit down, move to the front of the podium, walk to the side of the stage, force the audience to notice you—to look at you.
3. Use the chalkboard or visual aids. Redirect the group to a point where you want them.
4. Ask direct questions of the more disruptive group members.
5. Summarize or remotivate.
6. Change the volume or tone of your voice.
7. Call a recess or break.

Problem 4. The group gets off the topic

Solutions
1. Restate your objectives.
2. Summarize.
3. Ask yes/no questions, follow with why, then relate to topic or objectives.
4. Use your presentation aids or an illustration board.
5. Ask for the trainees' views.

SECTION V

STEP 4
EVALUATING

STEP 4— EVALUATING

Understanding the Applause

Evaluation is the final part of the instructional design. After you've learned how to plan, prepare, and conduct your presentation, you have reached the moment of truth. How well did you perform, how well did your presentation meet your stated objectives?

While preparing your presentation, keep in mind the need for evaluation. To determine the effectiveness of your presentation, you must be able to gain some immediate impression of your audience's retention of the material you present. This can only be done if you have good learning objectives, obvious main points, and clearly formed, desired learning outcomes.

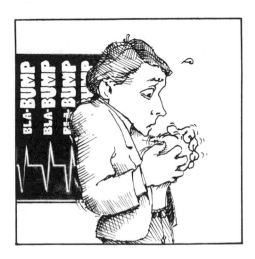

NO REASON TO FEAR EVALUATIONS

TESTING FOR RESULTS

Most people think of testing or evaluating as a series of questions. Questions may be of the essay, true-false, multiple choice, completion, or matching type. There are many more creative ways of evaluating your audience without administering a formal written exam.

Some of these include:

1. Performance or a demonstration

2. Structured role-playing in a case study

3. Group projects

4. Group or individual problem solving

5. Open discussion in a seminar format

6. Small group questioning and discussion

Performance is most appropriate for situations in which you are training for a manual skill such as the use of a personal computer. Manual skills also include behavioral activities such as leadership development or even acting. In these situations you can ask the trainees to demonstrate the use of the equipment in question, execute the behavior, or, in the case of teaching and leadership, demonstrate the behavior with surrogate trainees. In the latter case, however, role playing may be more useful.

Group projects are appropriate for subjects such as report preparation techniques. In these situations ask the trainees to cooperate as equals in the solution of a common problem. Each group member makes a contribution, although you may select a group leader responsible for preparing the report and presenting it to you and the other members.

Group or individual problem solving differs from the previous activity, group projects, in the nature of the problem. Here, all members of the group focus on a single, rather limited problem while in other cases each student takes a separate part of the larger overall problem to solve. A roundtable panel discussion is one appropriate mode you might use. All panel members contribute ideas and the group comes to a single solution.

Open discussion in the seminar format must be led by you, the facilitator. In this type of evaluation, you draw each trainee out one at a time by asking specific questions. You bear a heavy responsibility since you must be prepared to ask each trainee several questions if the conversation doesn't continue. The flow of the logic you use must both be interesting and stimulate a trainee to cover the proper scope of the question. Your major objective is to start and fuel a dialogue with trainees—the more animated the better—so that they tell you how much they have learned.

Classroom or small group questioning is a slightly more formal variation of the seminar format. In this case you do not rely on the trainees to fuel the conversation. You must be prepared to pose more than one question to each trainee. You will need to use this more frequently in the early stages of your presentation. The group may be reluctant to talk and volunteer information and ideas. After they become more comfortable with your topic, you, and the other participants, they can and should be guided into the open discussion format.

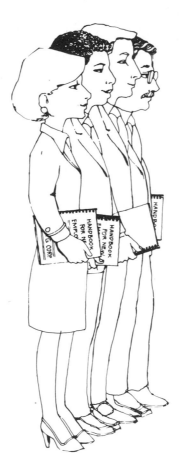

SECTION *VI*

SUMMARY AND REVIEW

SUMMARY AND REVIEW

Sit down as soon as possible after each training session and again develop the training outline the way it was presented. Jot down what your first reactions are to the program and then record the sequence of the content and explain what processes occurred. Record the good points, disasters, what caused laughter, and note tense spots for you or the audience.

Reread your notes some time later away from the training situation, and then carefully go through the steps you took to develop your design and the elements of your lesson plan. Edit, make adjustments and annotations, and rewrite critical parts if you intend to use the same lesson plan again.

Last but not least: make a short list of things you'd hate to forget to do the next time you start this whole process!

Good instructional designs make for successful programs and trainers.

Good luck!

NOTES

FOR OTHER FIFTY-MINUTE SELF-STUDY BOOKS
SEE THE BACK OF THIS BOOK.

NOTES

FOR OTHER FIFTY-MINUTE SELF-STUDY BOOKS
SEE THE BACK OF THIS BOOK.

ABOUT THE FIFTY-MINUTE SERIES

We hope you enjoyed this book and found it valuable. If so, we have good news for you. This title is part of the best selling *FIFTY-MINUTE Series* of books. All other books are similar in size and identical in price. Several books are supported with a training video. These are identified by the symbol **V** next to the title.

Since the first *FIFTY-MINUTE* book appeared in 1986, more than five million copies have been sold worldwide. Each book was developed with the reader in mind. The result is a concise, high quality module written in a positive, readable self-study format.

FIFTY-MINUTE Books and Videos are available from your distributor or from Crisp Publications, Inc., 95 First Street, Los Altos, CA 94022. A free current catalog is available on request.

The complete list of *FIFTY-MINUTE Series* Books and Videos are listed on the following pages and organized by general subject area.

MANAGEMENT TRAINING (Cont.)

PERSONNEL/HUMAN RESOURCES

COMMUNICATIONS

CUSTOMER SERVICE/SALES TRAINING (CONT.)

SMALL BUSINESS/FINANCIAL PLANNING

ADULT LITERACY/BASIC LEARNING

CAREER BUILDING

To order books/videos from the FIFTY-MINUTE Series, please:

1. **CONTACT YOUR DISTRIBUTOR**

   or

2. **Write to Crisp Publications, Inc.**
   95 First Street   (415) 949-4888 - phone
   Los Altos, CA 94022   (415) 949-1610 - FAX